Swampy Mess

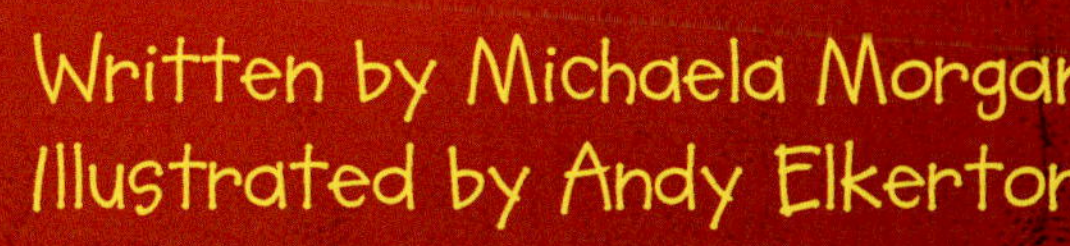

AF604719

Written by Michaela Morgan
Illustrated by Andy Elkerton

Horribilly is a ...

BIG...

soggy...

green and gloopy...

monster.

He is the only monster at Golden Pond School.

Horribilly can be a bit clumsy.

"What can I do to show I'm sorry?" said Horribilly.

“Let’s put on an art show,”
said Horribilly’s friends.
“People will pay to see the show.
Then we can get a new chair!”

“I’ll do a painting of my home in the swamp,” said Horribilly.
“I want to do an extra **SPECIAL** painting!”

He began sploshing paint and singing,

"A splash of red, a blob of blue.

Add a dab of yellow, too.

Lots and lots of swampy green,

for the swampiest painting you've ever seen!"

The paintings were very good.
But Horribilly wasn't happy.
"Something is missing," he said.
"It's not very swampy."

The teacher put up a poster.

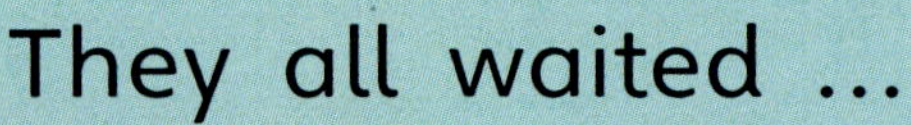

They all waited ...

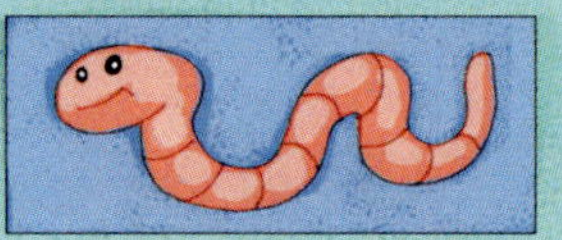

and waited ...

and
waited ...

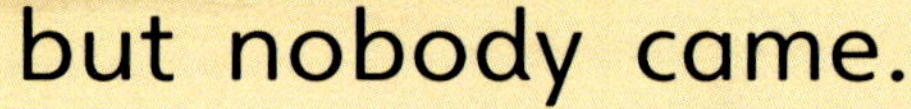

but nobody came.

Horribilly was sleepy.
Oops!
Splash!
Oh no!

Horribilly ran to save his painting.
Dab dab dab he went ...
and rub rub rub he went ...
and scrub scrub scrub.

"Oh no!" said Horribilly.

He ran to get a mop ...

but he ran into the poster, too.

"Look at this mess!" said Horribilly.
"I'm very, very sorry."

Just then, people came into the hall.
"We are here for the art show,"
they said.
"The footprints led us here."

"So do you, Horribilly," said his friends. "You are extra special, too!"